By Sir Osbert Sitwell

LEFT HAND, RIGHT HAND!

THE SCARLET TREE

GREAT MORNING!

LAUGHTER IN THE NEXT ROOM

ENGLAND RECLAIMED AND OTHER POEMS

ENGLAND RECLAIMED
and Other Poems

ENGLAND RECLAIMED

and Other Poems

AN ATLANTIC MONTHLY PRESS BOOK

LITTLE, BROWN AND COMPANY · BOSTON

1949

FIRST EDITION

Published November 1949

ATLANTIC–LITTLE, BROWN BOOKS
ARE PUBLISHED BY
LITTLE, BROWN AND COMPANY
IN ASSOCIATION WITH
THE ATLANTIC MONTHLY PRESS

PRINTED IN THE UNITED STATES OF AMERICA

To Edith

CONTENTS

PART II: Foreign Parts

PART III: Poems of the Wars

THE book which follows, *England Reclaimed and Other Poems,* skims, or summarizes, in its present condition, thirty years of writing poetry: though years by no means continuous, for often the Muse of Prose has summoned me away for a long period by sounding a blast on her massive golden trumpet, but always have I returned. Nevertheless in the concentrated state in which it appears here, this volume was born of the five, to me, memorable and enchanting months which my sister and I spent recently in the United States, and of the readings of our own poetry which we gave in various cities there. Indeed, it is faithful to these readings, even to the degree that it begins with the item with which I most frequently opened my part of the program.

This poem is one of many portraits, entitled "England Reclaimed." Surprisingly, albeit Chaucer, the first great poet in our language, initiated poetic portraiture, it has not often been essayed in English and American poetry. To the portrayal of my own gallery, I brought a belief in the peculiar truth to be found in the foreshortenings employed by Breughel the Elder, and in the zest of his vision; I attempted similarly to visualize intensely, for others as well as for myself, the appearance of those I wanted to describe, and through their outward aspect and the rhythm it in turn imparted, to depict their personalities, their souls.

This record I made in an attempt to preserve for posterity their likeness, and still more to commemorate a tradition which was even then fast disappearing, and has since vanished. Such a way of life could have been matched a generation or two before, in various parts of the States: though there, too, it has gone utterly. . . . But indeed, these poems have another link with America, for I wrote many of them in the months following my first visit to New York and to Boston in 1926–1927. I suppose the distance at which I was then living from my home, and the very different life I saw round me, made me reflect, somewhat nostalgically, on those old friends I had known at Renishaw; and subsequently evoked these eclogues. But, in addition, the two readings I gave at that time in New York, of my own poems, much influenced my manner and the way in which I wrote them; for the experience thus briefly acquired had shown me how much poems varied in that particular quality which enables them to be read aloud: an attribute to which I began to attach a greater importance than do many other contemporary poets. It was to me as urgent a matter that a poem should be able to be read aloud with all possible effect, as that it should look well on its printed page. All those particular poems were written with both aims equally in view.

I have said already that each period of my poetic work is represented in this book. In it, the last written poem is "A Rose in the Mouth": while the first is the final poem in the volume, "The Next War." Prophecy should always be seen looking over the poet's shoulder, and this last poem has a singular history.

It was included in the first book of poems by my hand alone (I had already appeared jointly with my sister): but many months before this volume was published in England or America, Witter Bynner was kind enough to send me some cuttings relating to this poem (he had later found out it was by myself) from Californian newspapers. It is a long time ago: but one such extract is before me now, and explains itself, though the title of the journal is lacking. It is dated Berkeley, December 28th, and runs:

UNKNOWN POET SCORES WAR.
STANZAS FOUND ON MENU
GOOD VERSE, SAYS BYNNER

A poem scribbled on a grease-spotted menu in a San Francisco café bears so obviously the marks of genius that prominent authors and critics are today looking for the author of the unsigned verses. The owner of the copy received it from a French waiter on the night of the peace celebrations. . . . Bynner says that in the technique and word selection, the unknown writer shows himself to be a master of his art. The only mark of identification is the letter M. The title is "The Next War."

The poem was correctly quoted. . . . As for the initial M, it may have been a shortening of *Miles*, under which name my satires were invariably printed in the *Nation*,[1] during and after the war, until I was quit of the Army. . . . Even then, however, the odd destiny of this poem was not fully accomplished. . . . Some twenty years later, when it had become plain that we were on the verge of the war its lines had predicted, it was published in the columns of the *Nation's* successor and descendant, the *New Statesman and Nation*.

OSBERT SITWELL

May 10, 1949

[1] The English paper.

Part One

ENGLAND RECLAIMED

EXPLANATION

When men were children, and each race was young,
The praise of many a hero, bravely sung,
Resounded through each honeycombèd rock
In bee-like droning, smote with sudden shock
The mountain top, where in green-tufted tent
By sweetness drowsed, the shepherd breathes the scent
Of poignant herbs, outprest by scrabbling goat
That quavers to him in a voice remote
As laughter of old men. He stirs not. Past
Him floats the song, to brush the golden mast
Of full-rigg'd fruit trees, where they breast white foam
From fallen petals at their foot, to roam
Through echoing pastures, or invade the woods
Which now reveal, beneath receding floods
Of brutish blackness, goddess-trodden dells
And alleys, whence Apollo shade dispels
With level eye. All animal and furred
Had been that darkness, which with the first word
Man spoke to Man was quelled, by laughter banished;
And yet that fearful darkness has not vanished,
Still lurks within our blood — ape-haunted land
Where ev'ry Stone Age God can still command
With grunting utterance.

This chant of love,
This man-made music of the myrtle grove,
Was new then; in its cadence brooded Spring,
The sad months of miraculous blossoming;
Wherever shrilling water met green shade,
Within that laughing, leafy palisade
— As nightingales, that with a diamond tongue

Cut glassy darkness — first the poets sung.
No sooner in these havens had they trod
Before by song they made a Demigod:
All forms of music shared the sacred throne
And Priest and Poet could be seen for one.

. . . .

Heroic figures are now obsolete,
So Demigod and Devil find retreat
In minds of children — as rare beasts and men,
Elsewhere extinct, persist in hill or fen
From man protected — where each form assumes
Gigantic stature and intention, looms
From wind-moved, twilight-woven histories:
For them each flower teems with mysteries.
Thus poems, no less than mythology,
Are imaged through an inner, innocent eye
Preserved from childhood, of a vision clearer,
More true than truth, that brings each object nearer
And draws a strange strength from the hidden God
— For Poetry is the wisdom of the blood,
That scarlet tree within, which has the power
To make dull words bud forth and break in flower.

. . . .

The eye of childhood faithfully records
The destined figures creaking on the boards
Down alleys three — country, abroad and town —
The foreigner, the burgess and the clown:
A false perspective tricked t' appear more deep
Than those dark caskets in which now they sleep,
For children, as they grow, see Fate unfold
These puppets, pack them in their native mould.

. . . .

Now let us wake them: make Miss Mew sit up
To proffer us that kindly, wonted cup
Of tea, with "just a dash of green tea in it";
Her wrinkled laughter tinkles like a linnet
Among the tea-cups, pecks the ornaments
— The china-cats, the tinselled tournaments,
The ribbon work, which frames in blue and buff
Lord Beaconsfield, and Uncle's box of snuff,
The comrade in his circumnavigation
Of globes grown gay (this fabulous relation
Is often hero of preposterous tales,
Has raided slavers, and has tackled whales
In single combat). Green eyes open wide,
A white-hair halo foaming like a tide
About her gentle head, she finds escape
In tales of murder, piracy and rape:
Herself believes in these exciting stories
She blends of books she's read and memories,
The while sad mirrors of mahogany
Reflect one sequel to monogamy.
Let Mrs. Hague awake, to hunt her aitches
Down avenues which yet their flight enriches,
Each aitch a rustic goddess, with a crook,
That stirs to life within her green-cut nook:
Let that old soldier, Major Nicodeme,
Provide us with a braggadocio theme.
All these and others let us now implore
To rise, shake on their dust, and speak once more.
Before oblivion's creeping, greedy sea
Shall wash this dust away irrevocably
Beyond our reach, let us the past despoil,
Reclaim these precious yards of English soil.

PROLOGUE

Now watch these phantoms,
How they tremble into being,
Amble, tremble into ample phantoms,
Tumble into their small wants
– Such few desires,
Garden, food, fires.
Watch these phantoms
How they now are being,
Listening . . . . . . hearing,
Looking . . . . seeing,
Loving . . . . fearing,
While to tinge their moods, stiff-jointed moods,
The dumb, the sad, the sunset shadow
Of the old house broods.

Alas, again, the ample phantoms tremble,
Tumble and crumble out of their few needs –
Crumble . . . then crumple up.

MR. AND MRS. GOODBEARE

Elegy for Mr. Goodbeare

Do you remember Mr. Goodbeare, the carpenter,
Godfearing and bearded Mr. Goodbeare,
Who worked all day
At his carpenter's tray,
Do you remember Mr. Goodbeare?
Mr. Goodbeare, that Golconda of gleaming fable,
Lived, thin-ground between orchard and stable,
Pressed thus close against Alfred, his rival —
Mr. Goodbeare, who had never been away.

Do you remember Mr. Goodbeare,
Mr. Goodbeare, who never touched a cup?
Do you remember Mr. Goodbeare,
Who remembered a lot?
    Mr. Goodbeare could remember
        When things were properly kept up:
    Mr. Goodbeare could remember
        The christening and the coming-of-age:
    Mr. Goodbeare could remember
        The entire and roasted ox:
    Mr. Goodbeare could remember
        When the horses filled the stable,
    And the port-wine-coloured gentry rode after the tawny
            fox:
    Mr. Goodbeare could remember
        The old lady in her eagle rage,
            Which knew no bounds:
    Mr. Goodbeare could remember
        When the escaped and hungering tiger

Flickered lithe and fierce through Foxton Wood,
When old Sir Nigel took his red-tongued, clamouring
hounds,
And hunted it then and there,
As a Gentleman Should.

Do you remember Mr. Goodbeare,
Mr. Goodbeare who never forgot?
Do you remember Mr. Goodbeare,
That wrinkled and golden apricot,
Dear, bearded, godfearing Mr. Goodbeare
Who remembered remembering such a lot?

Oh, do you remember, do you remember,
As I remember and deplore,
That day in drear and far-away December
When dear, godfearing, bearded Mr. Goodbeare
Could remember
No more?

Mr. and Mrs. Goodbeare

MR. GOODBEARE's parlour was a paradise
Of polished wood, a haven of joinery,
A heaven of varnish.
There were brackets, shelves, shields
And cupboards, with ferns traced on them
By his artistry,
And even wooden vases, turned
So beautifully, and full of dried, dull grasses,
Tied with dusty ribbons,
That rustled suffocatingly

In the dry wind from under the door.
Fantastic flights of Mr. Goodbeare's imagination,
Cricket-bats combined with dragons,
And improbable bows and loops,
Framed-in the almost legendary
Topiary of beard and whisker –
Tied in True-lover's Knots,
In which Mr. Goodbeare's friends
Had at one time extravagantly –
If elegantly – indulged.

. . . .

Mrs. Goodbeare herself appeared no mean feat of turnery,
As she creaked into the room
In her best black satin dress.
The lines on her face,
Of hairy yellow wood just cut,
Had been incised, perhaps,
By Mr. Goodbeare's verbal saw,
Just as his actual one
Had roughly shaped her figure.
Carved from one tree-trunk
She appeared,
Save for a golden-gleaming tooth,
A weird, wild tooth
That flashed in sympathy or anger.

Mrs. Goodbeare was a diplomat
And played off Mrs. Hague 'gainst Mrs. Nutch –
Yet sometimes I feared that Mrs. Goodbeare
Thought that dear, bearded, godfearing Mr. Goodbeare
Remembered remembering
Too much.

Mr. Goodbeare at Work

UNDER the shade
Of the elder-bushes,
In the speckled glade,
Where the thrush-coloured toads crouch
About to spring,
Where the toad-coloured thrushes
Learn to sing,
To shake their notes
As do Prima-Donnas
From white, fat throats;
When the tulips flaunt
Their proud bandannas,
And the cuckoos haunt
Us with mocking hosannahs,
Then, if you pass
Betwixt orchard and stable,
You can hear the saw shriek
From the Carpenter's table.
With saw and with plane,
The colour of rain,
He turns the old trees into shelves; or, again,
Into hives for the bees
That seek golden ease
In the cups of the flowers
Battered down by the showers,
Blue-cold as the claw
Of the plane or the saw
That make for cattle a pen,
Or fashion coffins for men.

. . . .

But if Mr. Goodbeare
Planes the planks, and prepares
Caskets for men's skeletons,
Alfred for this atones,
And takes him unawares
By planting flowers
For Mr. Goodbeare's dry and tirèd bones.

Mr. Goodbeare's Cottage

How Mrs. Goodbeare
Could ever have contrived
In that Sahara of dry grasses and dry wood
To suffer "from rheumaticks somethink dreadful"
Remains her secret
— The only one which Destiny allowed her.
For Mr. Goodbeare, being a carpenter,
Enjoyed immensely the effect
Of windows,
                    Tightly closed
                                        And nicely, very nicely, painted,
Of well-turned wood,
                                    Well-seasoned,
And of painted putty
                                        (Oh, the painted putty!)
While the neatly-fitting panes
Afforded him an exquisite sensation,
Unknown but to his trade.
The glass panes gave a gloss
To anything behind,
And brought to mind —

French Polish,
Zenith of evolutional anthropoid achievement.
Then there were always plants,
An aspidistra or two, behind the ice
That shut them from the northern world.

Sometimes the windows looked
Like mountain waters rilling over ferns,
Sometimes the fleshy red lip of a cactus
Touched them to strange exoticism,
Or, again, the sun flashed down on one
Till it resembled
The golden tooth
That gleamed in sympathy or anger.

No air was there within –
Except the dry wind creeping
And squeezing and moaning and whining under the door
While the house was sleeping –
For no window was ever open,
Neither upon the glittering steel flowers of the frost,
Nor on those fantastic blossoms
Spun by the sun with aid of summer rain
Among most ordinary green leaves,
Nor on those magic crystal lilies
Which the rain beats up
Upon hard paths
And which dissolve and die in blossoming,
Nor ever on the cornucopia
Of summer noons weighty with full-blown roses,
When the Red Admirals ride smoothly

Down the painted tide of petals,
Furl their shuddering sails
Deep in the harbour of the flowers' heart –
But, for her, only on to valleys biblical,
Valleys that still were
The Church-of-England haunt and habitat
Of Baal and Jael
('Tis true the wooden pin
Excited *his* professional interest too),
Of flaunting, dizened Jezebel
And strings of generating names –
Nimrod, Omri, Melchisedek, Nehemiah:
For him, on to dry lawns of rattling, pressed grasses,
On to perspective-twisting pastures
Of the things remembered,
And now growing larger as they roll away
Toward the horizon, or upon
Desiccated forests of artful fretwork,
Or lone logs of wood, unseasoned and unpainted,
Still rooted in the earth –
Logs which would cut up beautiful
Into shelves: then into boxes, into frames,
Just dainty odds and ends,
So very handy, and the fruit of skill;
Meantime the unremembering, unambitious dove
Croons languorously
High up in Mr. Goodbeare's elm tree.

TOM

THE farmhand Tom, with his apple and turnip face,
Grumbles, grins and groans through the long summer hours,
Reviles St. Martin, by whose grace
Thus he must plod through the poppies and cornflowers.
Night is a stretch of dead and drear slumber,
Then up again, and again he must lumber
Into his clothes and away through the park,
Carrying pails,
Must wade through the dark,
Till even the comforting darkness fails,
Tousled and blinking,
Clanking and clinking,
A very robust
Traditional ghost:
For clanking and lank
The Armoured Knight
Rides down the dank
Shadows in flight;
Grass stiff with frost
Shows grey as steel
As the Conquering Ghost
Clanks down the hill.
Now the first cock crows,
Impudent, frightened, through the dark;
Then a cold wind blows,
And that whining dog, Dawn, begins to bark.
Then the Knight in Armour
Passes away,
As the growing clamour
Proclaims, "It is Day."

The trees grow taller,
The gate is shut.
The Knight grows smaller,
Goes smaller,
And out.

MRS. HAGUE

OLD Mrs. Hague,
The Gardener's wife,
Was not to be enclosed in any formulas.
She seems to stand upon a little mound
Of pansies,
            Primroses,
                        And primulas.
Outlined against the pale blue eye of northern spring,
Heavily planted in this printed muslin beauty
Of clumps and spots and dots and tiger-stripes,
She swelled with ideas and ideals of duty,
Emphatic,
          Rheumatic.

Mrs. Thatch,
The wife, she was sorry to say,
Of Lord X's gardener
— If such one could call him —
Was silly, town-bred, what Mrs. Hague would call
— Well, she really did not like to say it,
Did not know what to call it;
Shall we say a Ne'er-do-Well?
And all the time the primroses, the wind-flowers
Opened their eyes and pressed their nodding heads
Against her, and the moss seemed ready to
Run up those rugged limbs,
The lichen ready
To crystallize its feathery formations
Along these solid branches.

If not upon this flower-sprinkled mound,
Then Mrs. Hague stood
Pressed in the narrow framework of her door,
And fills it to our minds for evermore.
Out of the slender gaps
Between the figure and its frame,
Was wafted the crusty, country odour
Of new bread,
Which was but one blossom of the hedges
That Mrs. Hague had planted.

For Mrs. Hague was childless,
And so had wisely broken up her life
With fences of her own construction,
Above which she would peer
With bovine grace,
Kind nose, kind eyes
Wide open in wide face.
For

    Monday was Washing Day,
    Tuesday was Baking Day,
    Wednesday h'Alfred 'as 'is dinner h'early,
    Thursday was Baking Day again,
    Friday was a busy day, a very busy day,
    And Saturday prepared the way for Sunday,
    Black satin bosoms and a brooch,
    A bonnet and a Bible.

Nor were these all:
There were the other, more imposing, barriers
Of Strawberry Jam in June
And Blackberry Jelly in October:

For each fruit contributed a hedge
To the garden of Mrs. Hague's days.

These fences made life safe for Mrs. Hague;
Each barrier of washing, mending, baking
Was a barricade
Thrown up against being lonely or afraid.
This infinite perspective
— The week, the month, the year —
Showed in the narrow gaps
Between her and the door,
As she stood there in the doorway,
Narrow as a coffin.

> Oh, who can describe the grace of Mrs. Hague,
> A Mrs. Noah limned by Botticelli,
> 'Mid flowering trees, green winds and pensive flowers;
> A Rousseau portrait, inflated by Picasso;
> Or seen in summer,
> As through a tapestry
> Of pool, exotic flower and conifer?

As Daphne was transformed into a tree,
So some old elm had turned to Mrs. Hague,
Thick bole, wide arms and rustic dignity.

FIVE DRAWINGS OF MR. HAGUE

In the Park

No little mound,
                                        Printed with garlands of spring flowers,
Serves as a pedestal
For Alfred's memory,
But a bare hillock in a wooded park,
Where graze in clusters
The rouged and dappled deer
– With their large eyes and their thin ankles –
A miniature Stonehenge,
Of which green-aproned Alfred
Was the one vast monolith left standing;
A monosyllabic monolith;
For thirty years of childless married life
Had made him mute.
Alfred loved trees and silence,
And here Mrs. Hague
Dared not disturb him:
For, if Mrs. Hague's home was her castle,
Fortress of home-made jam and new-baked bread,
He ruled
                  The garden,
                                    Park,
                                                And potting-shed,
While the hothouse was a studio
In which he worked as artist,
And the peach-houses, the cucumber-frames
Were his also.

Vast monolith he stands,
A landmark many a mile off,
Surveying the trees,
Inspecting leaf and bark and branch –
    For Mrs. Hague
    Is not the only tree he loves:
    Had he wished, then,
    To turn her to a tree?
    Was it a love of trees,
    Or a hope of silence,
    That had once compelled him
    To an Apollonian pursuit of Mrs. Hague? –
Surveying the trees,
That stand up solitary and tall
Until, becoming rounder, smaller,
Across the fawn-soft slopes
They spin toward the far horizon,
Where foam the woods in green, receding waves –
Gay, singing woods,
In one of which was already growing,
Was, indeed, nearing its full growth,
The boarding for his large, his heavy, coffin.

In the Potting-Shed

Oh, for words with which
To paint him there from life,
As he stands in the potting-shed
    With the bass, like golden hair,
    And with his insignia,
    Scissors, basket and pruning-knife,
Amid a universe

Of unripe pears and golden bulbs,
    As the stove burns warmly,
    The stove crackles brightly,
And there is a smell of warm wood,
A warm wooden smell as of trees growing
    (Do not ask why the trees are growing,
        Do not ask why the trees are growing).

Here is harboured
The strength of the garden,
Enough growing-power
To make the whole country-side
Flicker
With the red and pink candles of the early spring,
And to illumine again
That little mound
On which for ever in our memories
Stands Mrs. Hague.

In the Hothouses

If Mrs. Hague belongs to *Primavera,*
It is to the winter,
A Flemish winter of snow and crackling iron twigs,
That one must assign Alfred.
But Alfred is a master of paradox;
When the English earth is cold
As the lama-ridden uplands of Tibet,
Its temperature subnormal, hungering
To take to itself the lately living, longing
To be warmed and fed
By the annual holocaust of influenza,

When the lake has sheathed its mirror,
And the white giant has put a glass in his eye,
When the shivering margins of the lake
Have wrapped themselves in the feathers of dead swans,
Then I open a glass door,
And in a crystal transparency,
As though within a block of ice,
I find Alfred
— Alfred, white Sultan,
Rajah Brooke of tropic isles —
In one of his dominions;
This one is a forest in the Congo,
A swamp in distant, pear-shaped South America,
The coast of New Guinea
And a jungle in Cochin-China.
    With crimson and damson
    The Nile and the Am'zon
    Emblazon
    This halcyon
    Of growing and blowing
    Warm blossoms and leaves.

The Spell

HERE the waves of Ceylon
Meet the breakers of the Archipelago —
Breakers trimmed with pearls
And with the eyes of dead sailors —
And out of all this is born
A grinning octaroon of a hybrid
    ("H'Alfred not 'imself to-day,
    Bothered about that 'ere new i-bread").

Here I find him,
Brain, huge stature, and artist fingers
Placed at the entire disposal
Of the most diminutive need
Of an almost invisible blossom.

Here, then, Alfred is a signed Van Eyck
Inserted in a Gauguin panel;
The perfumed and exotic steam
Distilled from Welsh coal —
Heir-at-law
To vast and prehistoric forests —
From African forests
And Papuan jungles,
Forms round his hairless head
The halo of a saint,
Or the contorted and mottled writhings
Of tropical branch and root
Crown him with Medusa's tresses.

(Can he, perhaps,
Turn Mrs. Hague to stone
As well as to a tree,
And thus make silence doubly sure?)

Fair and rather hairless
He is caught among the variegated tendrils
As in a cobweb,
While the hairy and gnarled arms
Thrust out toward him
Seem the legs of a gigantic,
Carnivorous spider,
Which ever drains his strength,
Consumes his years.

Impartially he would distribute praise
Among his turbaned favourites,
Garish or unobtrusive:
"Them's a lovely thing," he would say,
Indicating a novel invisibility
From the juncture of the Blue and White Niles,
Or pointing out some gargantuan magenta blossom
Newly arrived from the impenetrable forests of Brazil
"Them's a lovely new thing,"
And he muttered an incomprehensible spell
In horticultural Latin.

Discordant Dawn

WHEN the cock-crow stretches
The air tight as taut string
Of basso or violin,
Alfred washes and dresses
And hopes for an early spring.

Heavily,
        Warily,
Ever
        So cleverly
He treads through the garden
Where the cold night still lingers,
Though the gold salamander
Flickers its red-crested head
Above the hill yonder.
Now each sharp scent
Is doubly vehement,
Though the frost's white fingers

Pinch the thyme
And bruise the lavender.

An elephant,
                    Pendent
Over the frames,
Where the warm violets glisten
In mauves and magentas —
                                        The lips of Infantas —
In brick red or heliotrope,
The robes of Cardinal or Pope,
He murmurs their names
And the flowers listen.

Now a bonfire crackles,
Boldly flashing its golden comb,
Till the acrid scent
Of each frosty plant
Is lost in the firmament.

MARY–ANNE

1

MARY-ANNE,
Wise, simple old woman,
Lived in a patchwork pavilion,
Pitched on an island,
Feeding the piebald and the tartan ducks.

Flotillas of ducks
Lie low in the water,
And Mary-Anne seems
The Duck-King's daughter.
The floating ducks crack up in their arrow-pointed wake
The distorted, silent summer painted in the lake,
Till the days disappear
In a leaden stare.

Then Mary-Anne waddles
Through the evening cool,
And a smell of musk
Lingers by the pool,
For the trembling fingers of the honeysuckle
Wring out the blue and the dew-drenched dusk.

At night the pavilion
Is hung by a silver cord
That the nightingales plait
With their intercoiling song.
Within, Mary-Anne mutters
The Word of the Lord,
Till the candle gutters,

As the summer sighs outside
And taps
At the shutters.

2

The silver-threaded wire
With which the nightingales
Suspended her pavilion
Was not the sole support it seemed:
For there was a direct attachment,
An umbilical cord to Heaven.
Her web-footed world
Teemed with four-leafed clovers,
With tea-leaves, cards, new moons,
And every sort of augury.
Not frightened, never in the least,
But seeing things,
Constantly,
For was she not
The Seventh Child of a Seventh Child
Born under Venus,
Had she not seen the Blue Man ride
Away, the bleak night that the late lord died?

Opposite on the shore
Was the Cedar Avenue,
Where fallen fragrance hushed the footsteps,
And there,
Quite often of an evening,
Mary-Anne could see
The Cavalier lord walking,
More conventional in death than in life ever,

Carrying his handsome head beneath an out-turned arm.
It was he who had done all this for Mary-Anne,
Who had made the lake and given it countless things to mirror;
Who had made the broken flights of steps,
The balustrades, the floating-terraces
And colonnades, wherein Italian winds
Whispered and sang their arias —
Winds he had netted centuries ago
In the plumed grottoes of a Roman garden —
And statues that the years had fretted
To limbless, eyeless, lipless lepers.
It was he, too, who had planted the park with hawthorns
That prance like red and white chessmen
Through the chequered springtime.

3

In the winter her pavilion
Was a tent of swansdown.
The windows tightly closed
Showed through their brittle yellow ice
A fern, and cubèd walls.
The wild geese thrust their long necks
Out into the cold air above,
And the white feathers drifted up to the window.
Then the Family would come down,
Like so many cats after the birds, she always said.
The snowflakes would sway down,
And thud,
Thud,
Thud
Would sound the falling pheasants.

MR. AND MRS. NUTCH

Mrs. Nutch

DEEP in the summer wood
Under a patch of sky
Crouched Mrs. Nutch,
Sworn foe, harsh enemy
Of every cobweb, mouse and Roman Catholic:
Crouched Mrs. Nutch,
An ancient owl in spectacles,
An owl diminishing, alas, from year to year,
Slipping down out of sight
Behind the warm shelter of an apricot tree
    That billowed green leaves over golden stars.
For Mrs. Nutch and this tree,
Though she tended it
And it bore fruit for her,
Were marching in contrary directions.
The tree grew taller
As Mrs. Nutch grew nearer to the ground,
Whence one sprang,
And by which the other
Was soon to be swallowed up.

In the huge height of summer,
When the smell of hay
Wandered down the long lanes of the wood,
Banished the damp smell of the bracken;
When the long, triumphant evenings
Planted their scarlet banners
In the very citadel of the hostile night,
Then Mrs. Nutch would stand in the doorway,

While her spectacles flashed back
The sun's victorious adieu,
Or would peep over
The spires of the campanulas,
As the evening winds
Ring their blue and white carillons –
Bloated capitalist campanulas,
Which to prosper
She must feed with blood.

. . . .

Few were her recreations:
There was the Ebenezer Chapel –
Stony acropolis of every mining-village –
She could ponder, perhaps,
On the Pope of Rome
Or the Whore of Babylon:
Read a passage she had found
In the newspaper
Aloud to incurious Mr. Nutch:
Then there was a musical box that tinkled *Carmen*,
Combing out luxuriant tresses with its golden teeth,
And her own cracked quavering
Of the "Hallelujah Chorus" –
A treat, this one, for others
As much as for herself,
To be served out to children
Instead of cakes or sweets.
After it, she would lie back,
Panting, in her chair,
As an owl pants in a holly-bush.
Sombre fires flickered in her eye,
While she sat there exhausted:

And then, suddenly,
As an aeroplane takes flight,
She would soar again after a fluttering, lustrous cobweb.

Mr. Nutch

Mr. Nutch,
Brown-bearded bear,
Chased the scamps of boys through fruit trees.
"Scamps," he called them,
But it was a serious affair,
Breaking down the palings
And Stealing Property.
    Clumsily he would grab and ramble,
    Angrily he would dart and grumble,
    Heavily he would sway and shamble
        After the nimble boys.
He would stumble among the trees,
Full-branchèd apples
That sagged beneath their rosy swags,
Or crabs that trailed their bitter-sweet rockets
Across the crisp autumn air.

Bombardments of apples
And impudent laughter
Met Mr. Nutch
Where'er he might wander,
His crinkled boots crusted with crystals
Under the glittering cobweb-tangled autumn.
(Oh,
    If only Mrs. Nutch
        Could have tidied up the season,
        What a different autumn it would have been,

With its neatly piled pyramids of apples,
Sorted according to size and colour,
Even the branches graded,
Placed symmetrically
One above another,
The grass dry, well-aired
And of an even height!)

But, as it was,
There, heavily trudging,
Angry and out of breath
Mr. Nutch must grab and ramble
From one walled garden to another.
At his approach
The birds would flutter in the fruit nets,
Bump and struggle in the fruit nets;
Each small bird that pecked the honeyed heart
Of golden or grape-blushing plum,
Was in reality a vulture
Feeding on Mr. Nutch's entrails —
Mr. Nutch,
That Prometheus bound to an orchard.
But the birds would flutter and struggle,
For Mr. Nutch
Was the natural enemy of every bird,
However soft or gaudy-feathered,
Just as Mrs. Nutch
Was the sworn foe
Of every cobweb,
Mouse and
Roman Catholic.

Mrs. Nutch, Mr. Noyes and Myself

MRS. NUTCH's constant expectation
Of the second coming,
A pleasurable but revengeful picnic,
Where the proud were, perhaps, more to be degraded
Than the humble exalted,
Disturbed my nights,
Filled them with the lion-mouthed roarings
Of drums and trumpets.

And so I lay awake,
Hearing the owls
Hooting round in the darkness,
While ever so far away
A loud-pounding goods-train
Lumbered along the southern path to London –
Lumbered along, had I but known it then,
To the precise rhythm of Mr. Alfred Noyes' verse,
For every train at night
Sings its own song
As surely as a bird.

. . . .

Then silence,
Mr. Noyes had finished;
The owl still snored,
Deep, ever so deep
In the holly,
Heigh-ho! in the holly.

Mrs. Nutch in Her Arm-chair

No wonder she was tired, she thought,
Working her fingers off, as one might say,
Working her very fingers off,
Every day except the Seventh Day.
For, ancient owl in spectacles,
She must sweep down continually
Upon her rightful prey,
The velvet-footed, clockwork-moving mice
That tittered so teasingly
Behind the panelling
Upon the Sabbath
    (Oh, they knew, they knew),
Or she must organize a battue
Against the spider
In all his wicked, silky machinations.

Moping Fred

Fred Nutch,
The final though not favourite offspring
Of the warrior pair,
Would in himself have blended,
One supposes,
Two such royal strains –
    Male gun and female broomstick –
But such, emphatically,
Was not the case.
He would not sweep or shoot:
                                        Instead
He hid within the wood
Or *Read*
    Among the roses
        (Oh, you could see it in his face, you could),
    A process widely noticed, rightly recognized
As "Moping" –
                        Hence
                                "Moping Fred."

In a Nutshell

Young Nutch, They said,
Would never be the Man
His Father was:
Because
    He did not know how to manage,
Carried no weight
In Evidence against the Boys –

Straddling across the creaking limbs of ancient apple
  trees,
Hanging their coronals of laughter
Untidily among the branches
As they climbed and clambered
Up in green cradles, golden bowls of light,
Clashing their coronals against the tiding silver of the
  songs
Of birds that sang more easily again
Because of the deceiving voice of that Delilah autumn
Receiving them into the heart of her false spring –
Would not even help his Father
Pursue the scamps –
Scamps *he* called them –
Through the golden corridors of the orchard
(Clumsily Mr. Nutch must ramble,
Angrily and alone must grumble,
Heavily and alone must shamble
After the nimble boys) –
Would not slit open the soft,
Warm, silver stomach of a rabbit,
Though its faunal ears were matted with blood,
Would not crucify an owl upon a barn door
Or help the old man out in any way:
Was,
To put it in that tooth-splintering
Yet well-chewed platitude, a nutshell,
Too fond of Moping
And of Reading Books –
Charges synonymous
And polyonymous,
Almost as serious
As Breaking Down the Palings and Stealing Property.

MR. AND MRS. SOUTHERN

Mrs. Southern's Enemy

AT dusk it is –
Always at dusk –
I seem to see again
That grey typhoon we knew as Mrs. Southern,
Spinning along the darkened passages,
Watching things, tugging things,
Seeing to things,
And putting things to rights.

Oh, would that the cruel daylight, too,
Could give us back again
Dear Mrs. Southern,
Dear, selfless, blue-lipped Mrs. Southern.
Cross, mumbling and transparent Mrs. Southern,
With her grey hair,
Grey face,
And thinly-bitter smile,
In wide blue skirt, white-spotted, and white apron;
On the very top of her head she carried a cap,
An emblem of respect and respectability, while
As though she were a Hindu charmer of snakes,
Her hair lay coiled and tame at the back of her head.
But her actual majesty was really the golden glory,
Through which she moved, a hurrying fly
Enshrined in rolling amber,
As she spun along in a twisting column of golden atoms,
A halo of gold motes above and about her,
A column of visible, virtuous activity.
Her life was a span of hopeless conflict,

For she battled against Time,
That never-vanquished and invisible foe.

She did not recognize her enemy,
She thought him Dust:
But what is Dust,
Save Time's most lethal weapon,
His faithful ally and our sneaking foe,
Through whom Time steals and covers all we know,
The very instrument with which he overcame
Great Nineveh and Rome and Carthage,
Ophir and Trebizond and Ephesus,
Now deep, all deep, so deep in dust?
    Even the lean and arid archæologist,
    Who bends above the stones, and peers and ponders,
    Will, too, be his one day.
Dust loads the dice,
Then challenges to play,
Each layer of dust upon a chair or table
A tablet to his future victory.
And Dust is cruel, no victory despising,
However slight,
And Dust is greedy, eats the very bones;
So that, in the end, still not content
With trophies such as Helen of Troy,
Or with the conquering golden flesh of Cleopatra,
He needs must seize on Mrs. Southern,
Poor mumbling, struggling, blue-lipped Mrs. Southern,
For Dust is insatiate and invincible.

Twilight

THROUGH long and intimate association
With the objects under her protection,
Mrs. Southern had the air
Of being in league with inanimate objects,
Conspirator with chair and table,
Sentient wall, inquisitive-eyed portrait.

So, when I hear faint creakings from a board
Or in the twilight the muffled hurry and harry
And worry and flurry of something that scurries along,
I wonder what it is, and whether Mrs. Southern wanders
And works and suffers, yet bound to chair and table;
　　For she was always there,
　　Whenever you looked round.
　　She was there all the time:
　　Had been there the whole time
　　While you had called her:
　　Had been for fifty years,
　　Standing there, looking after things.

Is there, I wonder, is there in the guilty dust
Some indecipherable message
Written with accusing but invisible finger?
By a cruel fate, herself now actual part
Of that same foe she fought for a whole lifetime,
Surely she would betray him if she could,
As she watches him and his ally,
Night, the Black Panther,
Stealing on velvet paws
Through the long corridors,
Then slink into the garden where the red mouths tremble

Till all the points of colour crumble,
Till the young wind-god is woken
And battles with them as his muscles strengthen,
By his day-long drowsiness forsaken?
Now the glowing glass below is broken,
Now the plunging images are shaken,
And the dying shadows lengthen,
Lengthen,
Lengthen.

Mr. Southern in the Market Garden

MR. SAMUEL SOUTHERN, though he looked the part,
Toyed in no myrtle grove,
Nor was static in the forefront
Of any oriental landscape.
It is always on a summer day
(Then were no days
Save summer days,
Or a few days of swansdown,
When the old elms
Held high their hundred antlers,
Now spun of glass and silver,
Into the brittle blue of winter)
That I see him, sitting before a table,
Making up accounts in a vast book,
A local god, who blossoms on this stone platform
Beneath the shelter of a tulip tree,
Tallying life with death.
An emanation from the soil is he,
And yet a miniature god in his miniature heaven;
Behind him (the cloud posed for his godship)
Showed the gleaming, faded Orangery

Through whose mackerel-cloudy yet transparent scales
Could still be detected
(For chiming bells are due as much,
As much decreed, to minor gods,
As rolling guns for the salute of native princes)
The sad, pale ringing
Of a thousand waxen bells,
Gently swinging, nodding, ringing
High in the dark and leafy air.

There sat the god, and for the heaven he ruled,
Lay sprawled across the park, the old square garden
Full of the feathered trunks of apple trees,
Whose fluttered leaves ride, small cupids on a golden breeze.
Here Mr. Southern, rustic deity,
Could tot up to his satisfaction
The local lives and deaths,
The christenings, the marriages, the funerals
For which he customarily supplied –
According to th' inexorable laws
Of birth and death –
Or let us say of Supply and Demand –
Appropriate floral decorations.
And oh, he cherished a Shakespearian appetite
For every word of sexton and of verger,
And for each gesture of the undertaker!

No Flowers by Request

UNDER the apple trees
The garden was divided
Into four quarters,
Each box-edged and trim.
One quarter, thus, was given up to funerals,

And nominally one to christenings,
Though, actually, interchangeable,
Haunted by every damp, albino ghost
In its own season,
By all the decadent and spectral blossoms
From fainting snowdrop to the weak narcissus,
From fat, white daisies
To white asters,
While, worse than such moist ghosts
Were those dry, lifeless, stillborn, chilly flowers
That never can tremble and flutter as other flowers do like a bird on the breeze,
But can only quake and rustle and rattle.
And then, in a Good Year,
An influenza or a typhoid year,
He did a wun'erful lot o' trade,
He told me,
In white chrysanthemums —
Nothing like white chrysanthemums
To give the rich but cold look
That was wanted.

Then there was a quarter given up to weddings —
But a lot liked white for weddings too, Mrs. Southern for example —
And that final quarter for assorted flowers,
Suited to bazaars and jubilees,
Victorious wars and vicarage jumble-sales.
For these he recommended something patriotic,
Geraniums and lobelias,
With a touch
Of white . . .

PHOEBE SOUTHERN

Phoebe Southern

It was not
By Phoebe's hair of northern sunlight,
Weaving pale gold, pale green, all caught in gold,
That one would recognize her,
Nor by her figure
That like Daphne seemed
About to change into a lithe young tree
Of earliest spring, whose shrill green curls,
Unfolding like the purest melodies,
Are weighted down with coral buds and bells —
All swinging on the branches, gently ringing
In time with the deep-throated hornpipes,
The flings, the jigs and rigadoons
That are the favourite tunes
Of English birds, adventurous
Wave-braving mariners —
Nor by her green eyes' animal, swift flash,
Forswearing such arboreal temptation,
But by the crooning of her dove-like laughter,
That fluttering laughter,
Laughter of birds high up, content in their jade summer,
The laughter of a naiad,
As she flits like a dryad through the drowsing woods,
As she drifts down the orchards
With their anchored clouds,
Or across the lawns, like Leda for the moment
Enfolded, swallowed up in the flashing, frothing feathers
Of those proud swans, the fountains;
Still laughing is she,

Always questioning, always laughing,
Her voice carrying always, even in its laughter,
The upward-speeding, arrow-angle of a question.

Silver Lances

PHOEBE saw him as he tilted at the Turk's Head,
Riding low, stooping under the branches of the trees,
Half Robin Hood and half Crusader,
In his green uniform a-jingle with silver mail.

She saw him as he rode by at the gallop
Look toward her, turning in his saddle,
He had seen her and she saw him as he rode by at the gallop,
And the moving and the ripple of his chest now that his
    arm made ready
To tilt at the Turk's Head with his long lance of silver,
While in turn the sun tilted at him as he rode,
Tilting long shimmering lances down at him through golden
    branches.

It was
  After the Flower Show and the music and the uniforms,
  After the flowers, music and its furbelows,
    The changing sunlight and the waving trees,
  After the charging lancers with their lances flashing,
  After the tents, the booths and Punch-and-Judy shows,
  After the slow wandering, slow wondering,
  After the shifting and the tangle
    Of trees and flowers and tents and gaily moving
      people
    Upon the vegetable-scented, aphrodisiac breeze,

After the flashing brass and the heroic trumpets,
Swooping like gold-billed eagles down the wind,
After the conjuror and the rustic magic,
The green, the red and then the golden jangle
Of buzzing tunes amid the fluttering leaves,
That, laughing in the dusk, she met him,
That martial, moustached, stiff ghost of a coconut,
Sergeant Maypole,
With his matted hair and white teeth,
His wooden, hairy face and coconut-like muscles —
Though to her he was that glamorous crusader,
Romantic, amorous, Robin-Hood Crusader,
Set for eternity amid the music
Of trumpets under trees.

MR. AND MRS. KEMBLEY

Luke Kembley in September

The autumn was Luke Kembley's season,
October was Luke Kembley's month –
Though there was a lot to be said for September,
A nice fine September,
Hung with red apples and with golden pears,
A nice fine September,
Hung with glistening cobwebs;
A nice fine September,
When hilltop and meadow were full of the smell of the cabbage,
And when his stout shooting-boots
First plodded down the furrows
Of the fecund earth.

Stealthily crouching, he would stalk
Between the golden forts
And crenellated towers of summer,
Thrown up by the sweating binders
Against the invading Autumn –
For it was always a late harvest –
Between the leafy avenues of the root-crops,
Between the frozen waves
Of sea-green cabbages,
Off which the marble-veinèd dew would rattle,
As he passed,
Like the spray from breakers.
Sometimes his boot
Would crunch and crackle on a root,
As, later, would the strong teeth

And rhythmic jaws
Of the devouring cattle;
Then the plump birds would whir
Almost from beneath his foot,
Whir through the butterfly-hung air
With the rushing sound of an ogre's indrawn breath.

But in September
The Farmers were the trouble.
    Farmers were never contented,
        Farmers thought they had the right to everything,
            Farmers grumbled,
                Farmers took the law into their own
                    hands,
And you could not stop them:
So that,
    Though there was a lot to be said for September
        (A nice fine September),
October was Luke Kembley's month.

And October

October was Luke Kembley's month,
When the golden castles of the corn
Had been slighted by the roundhead autumn.
Then, red as the berries that grow
On the hawthorn hedges — oh!
He could walk after pheasants with a gun.

Day and night,
Spring and summer long,
He would lurk in the woods,
Eating bread and cheese

And never resting,
Preparing for October.
He would guard the sacred birds,
He would give them to drink,
He would offer up grain at their wooden altars:
He would even secure
Their effigies of straw
Within low branches,
So that,
            In the dark,
A panicked poacher
Could fire for ever at a sitting pheasant,
And no bird would fall.

In the night he would stalk the running sounds
Pursue the flickering lights:
Then the blue tapestries
      Would rustle sullenly, swaying
      Puffed out upon the breath
      Of the lank,
      The dank, green ghosts
      Of dead forests.
For
      October is the month,
      When the northern air is crystal
And the berries grow all red upon the hedges — oh!
When the tall trees grow antlers,
      And the three-prong'd leaves of the bracken
      Undulate on the pure air
      Just as the triple tails of imperial goldfish
      Wave through their transparent element;
      When even the Sun,

Magnificent Inca,
Wraps himself each evening
For his ceremonial farewell
In gigantic pheasant-feathers.
Then Luke Kembley's breath
Lingered behind him on the air,
As he walked back through the dusk
To find the sharp fingers of the fire
Gilding Mrs. Kembley
In the cottage on the hill.

But now through the cold and the long Octobers
The frost-flowers grow on the stiff stone borders,
And the dark winds blow
Through the lepers' window,
And the Parson blows his nose
As he passes in,
And the sky above
Is as dull as sin —
And the poachers trample down the dying woods,
And the pheasants are few,
The pheasants are few.

Circles

THE very house seemed circular,
A beehive or a top,
While Mrs. Kembley
Was not merely wife
To Mr. Kembley –
Far, far more than that.
Her very face and build and engineering
Shouted her "Female" to his "Male":

The same concentric circles,
    Highly coloured,
But used quite differently,
Arranged so dexterously,
Turned out into two lots,
Two continents,
Connected by a scarcely visible isthmus;
Or she might be an hour-glass,
    With a head above it.
So round was she, upon her two small feet
She seemed to spin, spin more than move,
Among the watery pleasances of her kitchen,
While beyond the open door,
Out in the garden,
    That lay scratched upon the hilltop
    Like a pattern made with a stick upon the sands,
All the flowers were either round and sweet
    And highly coloured,
Or, gently feathered like a pheasant,
Spun upon a pleasant breeze.

Interior of "The Boulders"

THE house was fortunately warm, a wigwam
Woven of fur and feather;
Had it been cold,
It would have been a mortuary,
A morgue for every feather, fur and fin.
There were feathers in vases,
Feathers in patterns hung up on the walls,
Feathers under glass,
And a feathered fire-screen.
Even the flames that this screen caged
Became diabolically mimetic,

And shook gay feathers from the grate,
Unfolded plumy tails.
Then there were innumerable fragments, finely mounted,
Of the beasts of the field as well as of birds of the air,
And huge fishes, with their fixed bright eyes,
Like those of paralytics,
That could yet contrive to catch,
From their glass houses,
Which boasted imitation reeds and ferns,
The bird-quick eye of Mrs. Kembley,
As she spun, bustled, opened and shut the doors.
Indeed, they swam right up the walls,
And mouthed aridly at her from the frieze;
While outside, in the kitchen, in the airy larder,
Through which there ever flew
A shrill, blue-feathered, little Alpine wind,
Were more birds, more dead birds,
Real birds, tied by their coral feet to rails,
More fish, all shining, damp and speckled,
Chequered or mail-coated,
With a piteous fin yet twitching,
Cradled in green rushes and long grass,
Just as they were brought in —
Rushes and green grass that cruelly parodied
Those green, faint-waving weeds
That had been shade
For all their glittering courtships,
Those weeds that rippled in the stream's clear play.

(This parody consisting
In the want of movement
In things that should, it seemed,
Move naturally and imperceptibly:
Just thus is death the parody of sleep.)

But Mrs. Kembley spun about
And bustled through her mortuary,
Her small feet tapping out
Quick staccato patterns on the hard, stone pavers;
There was much to do —
And the sound of the golden threshing
Was borne up from the field below.

Evening

Of an evening, Mrs. Kembley
Would wait for Mr. Kembley on the hill –
Waiting a little frightened,
For the woods under were so still,
So still,
For the mist crept up the nearer valleys,
Whispering white and chill;
Down in them something murmured
(Was it the distant rill?),
More dusky grew the long green alleys,
And the voices of the woods stabbed, sharp and shrill.
Then the nearest light winked yonder,
Miles down, by the mill,
And the Roman road ran straight and silent,
Empty and waiting, it seemed, along the hill.
She knew there was no reason to be frightened,
There was nothing for her to fear.
The valleys thus were always whitened
By the mist; the cruel wood voices sounded shrill
Always when all else was still —
But darkness was sidling near,
And nearer,
And Mrs. Kembley waited on the hill. . . .

MISS MEW

A Feather Tapestry

How few
The things we knew
About Miss Mew!

She was a delicate feather blown out of a pastel past,
Upon some shattering gale
Of which no one was ever told the nature.

There had been a gap, a long gap, and then
Pitching upon some dull, some blunt
Relentless gust of the east wind
She had drifted hither,
This delicate feather;
Here, where the waves ruffle their white plumage
At her all the winter,
Here, where the sky brushes the blue tops of the houses
All the winter
With its grey feathers, black or yellow feathers.

Age could not undermine her grace,
But only fashioned her more lightly,
Gave her a white halo,
And made her green eyes larger
In her white, small face,
So lightly carved her feet, that when she walked,
She drifted like a feather adown the wind,
Drifting among these other brutal and gigantic feathers
That buffeted and battered her
In the unreal and yellow light of English winter.

Miss Mew-ad-Vincula

WHAT chains, then, what weights were there
To bind her down
— This feather floating on the wind —
To the substantial winter of her life?

An undefinable, slight accent in her speech,
Drifting down it lightly as a feather in the wind;
No education and much knowledge;
A carriage accident, political convictions;
A love of stage and dancing, and of scenes
Where under the green and sickly flicker of the gaslight
Pranced Taglioni on her bird-swift toes
Leading a floating and angelic host
Of swooning swans and pirouetting nymphs;
Allegèd friendship with the hook-nosed Gounod
Among the painted pinks and blues,
The pampered but rebellious palm-trees
Of the early Riviera,
So that to our minds
All the trinkets in her house
Tinkled when she spoke or moved
To the rhythm of the Jewel-Song;
And that rare atmosphere which she distilled in talk,
An atmosphere both bourgeois and bohemian
Combined of high-kicks and home-truths,
Flirtation, elegance, and laughter,
But with the gilded pawnshop and the golden ginshop
Always around the fogbound corner,
A world of dead decorum, heavily haunted
By the charcoal spectres of Mr. Mantalini and Professor
    Turveydrop;

The fact that she had seen a whale
Washed up at Yarmouth;
And, strangest weight of all,
Her oft and loudly boasted declaration
That she had taken in the *Daily Mail*,
Each day since the *Daily Mail's* beginning.

Miss Mew's Window-Box

THE window-box, ever so high up,
Floating above the grey sea,
Crowded and clustered with brown, speeding wings
Was all the garden that Miss Mew possessed.
But this small coffin of earth
Was a whole world of life,
Flickered always with the brightly coloured buttons,
The sugar-sticks, rosettes, and candle-flames
Of early spring,
Or with the ragged cockscombs and the fuller bonfire —
flamings
Of the Autumn, trampling with its wild, golden hoofs:
For Miss Mew's calendar, just like her life,
Confessed to no high summer.

Over this oblong world,
Half-coconuts swung like hairy stars
In a miniature tarred gale from off the sea,
While cotton-wool-coated, coral-footed birds,
Acknowledging Miss Mew as feathery peer,
Pricked out a wooden music with their beaks,
Tapping against the various surfaces,
Or sent up little silver jets of song

Spurting against the crystal pane,
Or flew down on soft wings
With one wing quivering and bumping
Against her window, till she threw it up,
Her nimble fingers fluttering among the flowers,
Dispensing fruit and breadcrumbs.

. . . .

But now the paint is off the window-box,
There come no flowers either in spring or autumn,
No sugar-sticks, rosettes or candle-flames,
No ragged cockscombs and no fuller bonfire-flamings.
The birds bump up against the window,
Staring like a vacant, bleary eye,
Bump wildly up against the window
As though they wished to fly in through the dark emptiness:
And warmly buried in the now flowerless earth
Where others lie so cold and still,
The worms wriggle and snigger at their triumph,
Now the nimble fingers are no more nimble,
And the silver thimble lies cold and tarnished black.

MRS. KIMBER

Invocation

ALL hail,
    Ever borne back to mind
    On any salt and stinging wind
    That grows a rind
    Of tar!

All hail,
    Blythe spirit of the uncomplaining North
    (For such was Mrs. Kimber,
    Dear, dwindling Mrs. Kimber
    With her quick, crenellated smile
    And simple speech
    That yet could never fail
    In metaphor and image),
Yes, all hail, all hail!
See, she approaches;
There's her tartan shawl!
We must find a suitable accompaniment
For her appearance;
    Let, then, no dancing, light-foot waves
    Of southern seas, however azure-lined
    And tipped with swansdown,
    Their pale sands
    Paven with pavonine and roseate shells
    And parian limbs of gods and goddesses,
    With cups of Bacchus and with ears of fauns,
    Supply their trivial music for her.
    But, instead, sound forth
    Loud cacophonious breakers of the North,

Fringed with grey wings of seagulls,
Lined with black, slimy seaweed
And the bones of men.
You, too, you mournful bells,
Toll out from upright steeples
Of English seaside towns;
Sound your twin tongues,
St. Peter and St. Paul,
Toll out, St. Thomas and St. Saviour,
St. Ethelburga and St. John,
ALL,
ALL!

Mrs. Kimber

WHEN the sea was smooth
— Hilly, that is, not mountainous —
Tolling bells could not depress her.
At night asleep,
And busy, very busy, all the day,
Bustling and dusting,
She was blythe and gay,
Singing like a kittiwake about her work
By the first light,
So greenly submarine,
That filtered in at frosty windows
— And this held equally at bay
The spectres of the past and future,
Spectres of the deep.
She lived, or seemed to live,
In an old house, so flashing white
It might be carved from salt,
That tilted down a hill,

Ribbed, herring-bone-like, with red tiles.
And here she tended
Her four stout sailor sons
And darned and mended
(Darned and mended).
Often away,
One upon each of the four seas,
She kept things ship-shape for them
—Even when at home
Life was conducted
To the sound of bells,
The very rhythm of the sea,
While their rolling gait
Brought the victorious rush of waters
Into the timid, solid streets of houses.

Thus she was ever busy
On her sons' behalf,
Scrubbing floors,
Polishing glass-cases, kettles,
Washing doors,
Cutting spikes off urchins,
Whitewashing the yard
—Where pointed jawbones of a whale or two
Supplied triumphal arches for their valour;
And wherein,
Caught by her youngest,
Flopped and flapped a seal,
With the same sudden smile as Mrs. Kimber's.
"Like a cat for fish, that sea-calf,"
She would remark,
Applauding kindred zeal.

Properties and Prospects

This was her life, one thought
(Dear Mrs. Kimber, whose quick machicolated smile
Still haunts me);
A busy life in rooms low-roofed,
Crowded with ostrich eggs, large spiky shells,
And coloured views of foreign parts
Prisoned in glass paper-weights,
And little ships in bottles.
Then there were ornaments of jet,
And, hanging on the wall,
The Queen, on her two jubilees
(Head resting on imperial hand),
Some brittle bunches of white seaweed
By which to skill the weather,
And from each window
An abruptly falling street
Edged with wide seas;
While, as the prospect from the windows of her soul,
There stretched an acrid, waterproof perspective
Of fishing nets and bibles,
Red sails, red-herrings, kind tarpaulin faces,
All washed by a sea of soap-suds,
With Sunday as a weekly, workless culmination,
A formal day of dreams and how-d'you-dos,
Of boots like irons, violets in a bonnet,
And, just visible beyond this barrier,
Gigantic anti-climax of the usual Monday,
Dim, workaday Monday
Set in a golden cloud of whirling dust.

But often
(When the seas were smooth)
Mrs. Kimber was not there at all,
Floated out of her surroundings
Into an ideal world;
A scaly universe, with Aberdeen,
Distant and unattainable metropolis
Of fishing nets and shawls,
As its most fishy centre.
She could almost hear them, almost smell them,
Flopping alive upon the granite quays,
Almost see them, wriggling mountains
Of speckled gold and mottled silver, mostly silver,
Emptied from the trawlers,
To be appraised by expert eyes,
And pinched by expert fingers.
Gleaming, writhing hills of herring, cod and codling,
Ling, sprat, in their season, sole, smelt and whiting,
Plaice, lait, dab, trout and salmon,
Gurnet, pennock, wuff and billet,
Thornback, Monk Fish (or Sea Devil),
Eels, conger eels and sand eels,
Cuttlefish, Black Jack and Old Fishwife.
"Fish," she would say, "is in my very bones."
And so it was: she knew the names of them,
So very many fishes,
And their story,
Their times and seasons,
When to catch 'em, when to cook 'em
(Almost, one felt, she comprehended their last wishes),
How the moon affected mackerel
And the stars, a dory.

Rough Weather

But, when the sea was rough,
When the deep sound of bells
Was smothered in the gale
That cracked its whips
At every corner of the town,
When the thunder of the breakers
Pounded below, at cliff that crumbled,
Beneath the tearing cries of seagulls,
At once she'd quit her visionary world:
Then,
        Remembering her husband,
Her brain would turn all skimble-skamble,
And her eyes, flowers of the Northern waters,
Would strain toward the horizon,
Where the mountains shifted,
Watching, watching the seas whereon there sailed her sons;
Those Northern seas,
Lined with black, slimy seaweed
And the bones
Of men.

Toll from tall steeple,
Mournful bell!
But let
Your voice be caught, caught up and smothered in the wind,
So that it reach her not . . .
Not yet,
            Not yet.

Colophon

SEE how this stinging wind
Precipitates her in the mind,
A regular shape in crystal
Formed by the natural processes of chemistry!
See, there she sits now,
Beneath the ribboned portrait of her Queen!
Come, let us approach her:
We need fill
No beaker with the blushful Hippocrene,
But, while proud kettles puff their ostrich-plumes
And lids uprise upon a chanting gale,
From Indian herbs their sepia juice distil
And pledge her, crying again
All hail,
All hail!

GRAND FINALE

The Flower Show

IF I must leave the faces that I love,
Let it be when every dove
    Is crooning, swinging in the soft June trees,
And roses ride on every breeze:
    Thus would I love the faces that I leave
    And need not so much grieve.

Vast yellow mushrooms, tents are pitched
Beneath tall shadow-weaving trees
    That wring long hands
    And flutter their green fingers,
Amazed at so much boisterous hilarity,
While the grass, blue hair of wood-nymphs,
Displays broad yellow partings, leading to the tents;
Partings made yellow with the trip and tramp
Of boots, such stiff and torturing best-boots.
Now, in the yellow fungoid shade within,
So thick a crowd attempts to move
That all the bodies merging into one
Make movement slow and vastly ponderous —
    As though an elephant
    Both filled the tent
And strove to trample through it —
While this beast, more fabulous
    Than any howdah'd favourite
    Kneeling in grey salaam
Before some proud, some emerald-crested peacock of a
        Rajah,

Supports a thousand shifting heads,
Each with a bowler hat or bonnet
Jauntily perched upon it.
And all these faces, shining faces full of wonder,
Perpetually are shifting, blossoming anew
(And yet not only do these faces shift and blossom,
But some drop down each year,
Withered as though by magic, nothing left of them —
Only another youthful head blossoms more gaily
There, where the old one nodded for so long,
Not even a small gap now showing to record it),
And all these faces, shining faces full of wonder,
Open into fresh patterns of contentment,
As they peer and stare and let the scene
Drum through them, permeate them with its marvels;
Intent with both eyes and one ear,
For now the fanfare changes
To a rhythmic drone;
The other ear is bent to catch
The succulent spirals of the tune,
Sea-fruit up-thrown against this littered shore
By the brassy ocean's snore.
Such tunes have lives as much as mortals,
For, just as gods breathe into men
The life that grows, then flows, then ebbs away,
Thus does a tune derive its life from man;
And this dead tune,
This empty, broken shell
Matches the relics that we see about us,
The bits of fur and feather, and the sequined
Finery of such a festival,
Where dance dead fashions with a clownish elegance

Through yellow air, scented symphonically
With hot red roses, with carnations,
Prize onions and prize potatoes,
In their various armours of gold, their armours of purple,
With the smell of hairy, yellow boards
Pressing down upon hot, yellow grass.
And through this gloom, and through the blatant sounds
Of unearned and departed glory,
The warm, contented faces
Smile, speak a word, or hang above
The bouquets and the nosegays and the posies
That wilt in jampots and inferior vases,
Carefully consider horticultural triumphs
    That singly ride
    In pride as specimens.

Among these happy hanging gardens
Of red and rustic faces,
    Which hide few fancies
    And are round and open as the pansies
That tied in little crumpled velvet bouquets
Curl up their petals, there are many that we know.

But, as the flowers in the yellow tent,
These bouquets, and these nosegays and their posies,
Wilt, hour by hour, in their inferior vases,
So wilt and wither these poor, happy heads, now bent
Above the blossoms, year by year.
And as they stoop, and bend, and form their judgment
With careful and appraising eye,
So, surely, for a moment I could see
God's face bent down, and peering curiously

Above these faces, wide and open as the pansies'
Faces, which have no doubts, and hide no fancies.

If I must leave these faces that I love,
And it is not when every dove
Is crooning, swinging in the soft June trees,
And roses ride on every breeze,
Then let me take of them my last farewell
At this sad, this gay, this flowery festival;
So would I love the faces that I leave
And need not so much grieve.

Sound out, proud trumpets,
And you, bugles, blow
Over the English Dead,
Not slain in battle, in no sense sublime
These rustic figures caught at last by Time,
And yet their blood was warm and red
As any roses that in England grow
To these anonymous armies of the dead.
Blow, bugles, blow;
Sound out, proud trumpets, let your brazen thunder
Wake them to make them pass
Before us under the wide sky.
Thunder, drums and trumpets, thunder,
Wake them, to rise from where they lie
Under,
Under,
Under
The green grass,
Under the wide grey sky.

Part Two

FOREIGN PARTS

THREE MEXICAN PIECES

Dusk

NIGHT like a hawk
Swooped down
Onto the phoenix bird,
— Tore out its flaming feathers.
Solitary plumes
Flared, falling through darkness,
Floating above the distant sea.
Stillness and heat clung together
And the hawk
Spread out her wings.

Gigantic pinions
Flutter the air above,
Fanning our faces
And
We sing . . .

Song

Ah! Que bonitos
Son los enanos,
Los chiquititos.
Y Mezicanos.

OLD MEXICAN SONG

How jolly are the dwarfs, the little ones, the Mexicans,
Hidden by the singing of wind through sugar-cane!
Out comes the pretty one,
Out comes the ugly one,
Out comes the dwarf with the wicked smile and thin.

The little women caper and simper and flutter fans,
The little men laugh, stamp, strut and stamp again,
Dance to the bag-pipe drone,
Of insect semitone,
Swelling from ground slashed with light like zebra skin.

The Little Cardinal, the humming-bird, whose feathers flare
Like flame across the valley of volcanic stone,
Fiery arrow from a rainbow
That the armoured plants have slain, low
Stoops to watch the dwarfs as they dance out of sight.

Hair, long and black as jet, is floating yet on amber air
Honey-shaded by the shadow of Popocatepetl's cone,
Their fluttering *reboses*
Like purple-petal'd roses
Fall through tropic din with a clatter of light.

The crooked dwarf now ripples the strings of a mandoline,
His floating voice has wings that brush us like a butterfly;
Music fills the mountains
With a riot of fountains
That spray back on the hot plain like a waterfall.

Smaller grow the dwarfs, singing "I'll bring shoes of satin,"
Smaller they grow, fade to golden motes, then die.
Where is the pretty one,
Where is the ugly one,
Where is that tongue of flame, the Little Cardinal?

Maxixe

Los enanitos
Se enajaren.

OLD MEXICAN SONG

THE Mexican dwarfs can dance for miles
Stamping their feet and scattering smiles,
Till the loud hills laugh and laugh again
At the dancing dwarfs in the golden plain,
Till the bamboos sing as the dwarfs dance by,
Kicking their feet at a jagged sky,
That torn by leaves and gashed by hills
Rocks to the rhythm the hot sun shrills;
The bubble sun stretches shadows that pass
To noiseless jumping-jacks of glass,
So long and thin, so silent and opaque,
That the lions shake their orange manes, and quake;
And a shadow that leaps over Popocatepetl
Terrifies the tigers as they settle
Cat-like limbs, cut with golden bars,
Under bowers of flowers that shimmer like stars.
Buzzing of insects flutters above,
Shaking the rich trees' treasure-trove
Till the fruit rushes down like a comet, whose tail
Thrashes the night with its golden flail,
The fruit hisses down with a plump from its tree
Like the singing of a rainbow as it dips into the sea.
The loud red trumpets of great blossoms blare
Triumphantly like heralds who blow a fanfare,
Till the humming-bird, bearing heaven on its wing,
Flies from the terrible blossoming,
And the humble honey-bee is frightened by the fine
Honey that is heavy like money and purple like wine,

While birds that flaunt their pinions like pennons
Shriek from their trees of oranges and lemons,
And the scent rises up in a cloud, to make
The swinging, hairy monkeys feel so weak
That they each throw down a bitten coconut or mango.

. . . .

Up flames a flamingo, over the fandango.
Glowing like a fire and gleaming like a ruby,
From Guadalajara to Guadalupe
It flies — in flying drops a feather,
— And the snatching dwarfs stop dancing, to fight together.

ON THE COAST OF COROMANDEL

ON the coast of Coromandel
Dance they to the tunes of Handel;
Chorally, that coral coast
Correlates the bone to ghost,
Till word and limb and note seem one,
Blending, binding act to tone.

All day long they point the sandal
On the coast of Coromandel.
Lemon-yellow legs all bare
Pirouette to perruqued air
From the first green shoots of morn,
Cool as northern hunting horn,
Till the nightly tropic wind
With its rough-tongued, grating rind
Shatters the frail spires of spice.
Imaged in the lawns of rice
(Mirror-flat and mirror-green
Is that lovely water's sheen)
Saraband and rigadoon
Dance they through the purring noon,
While the lacquered waves expand
Golden dragons on the sand —
Dragons that must steaming die
Of the hot sun's agony.

FROM CARCASSONNE

1

Now night,
        The sighing night,
Descends to hide and heal
The crimson wounds
Ripped in the sky,
Where the high helmet-towers
(With clouds as streaming feathers)
Have torn the heavens
In their incessant sunset battle.
Below,
    Upon the mound,
Small golden flowers
Release their daylight slowly
At the Night's behest,
Till they become pale discs
That quiver
When the evening wind
Draws his thin fingers
Down the dew-drenched grass
— As an old harper,
Who awakes
From drunken sunlit slumber,
Blindly plucks
His silver-sounding strings —
Making the sound
That, further, darker down
The trees make,
When they draw back
Their upturned leaves
In fountain-foaming hurry.

2

The curling, hump-backed dolphins,
Drunk with purple fumes
Of wine-stained sunset,
Plunge through the wider waters of the night —
Waters that well down every narrow street
In darkening billows,
Till they become quiet, full —
Canals that, mirror-like,
Reflect each sound
Of snarling song
In all the town.

And, as the dolphins dive,
There splashes back
Upon their goat-eared riders,
Dislodged in sudden fury,
The foaming froth of summer-cooling winds
— Issuing from where the northern trees
Bellow their resined breath
Across the seas
To ripple through far fields
Of twilight flowers —
Sweeping across
To where these old high towers
Of Carcassonne
Still stand to break their flow.

Neptune, from his high pedestal,
Can watch the waters of the night
Rise, further, further,
And the faun-riders sink below
The conquering, cool tide.

OUT OF THE FLAME

1

FROM my high window,
From my high window in a Southern city,
I peep through the slits of the shutters,
Whose steps of light
Span darkness like a ladder.
Throwing wide the shutters
I let the streets into the silent room
With sudden clatter;
Walk out upon the balcony
Whose curving irons are bent
Like bows about to shoot —
Bows from which the mortal arrows
Cast from dark eyes, dark-lashed
And shadowed by mantillas,
Shall in the evening
Rain down upon men's hearts
Paraded here, in southern climes,
More openly,
But, at this early moment of the day,
The balconies are empty;
Only the sun, still drowsy-fingered,
Plucks, *pizzicato*, at the rails,
Draws out of them faint music
Of rain-washed air,
Or, when each bell lolls out its idiot tongue,
When Time lets drop his cruel scythe,
They sing in sympathy.
The sun, then, plucks these irons,
As far below,

That child
Draws his stick along the railings.
The sound of it brings my eye down to him. . . .
Oh heart, dry heart,
It is yourself again.
How nearly are we come together!
If, at this moment,
One long ribbon was unfurled
From me to him,
I should be shown
Above, in a straight line —
A logical growth,
And yet,
    I wave, but he will not look up;
    I call, but he will not answer.

2

From where I stand
The beauty of the early morning
Suffocates me;
It is as if fingers closed round my heart.
The light flows down the hills in rivulets,
So you could gather it up in the cup of your hands,
While pools,
The cold eyes of the gods,
Are cradled in those hollows.
Cool are the clouds,
Anchored in the heaven;
Green as ice are they,
To temper the heat in the valleys
With arches of violet shadow.
You can hear from the distant woods

The thud of the centaurs' hoofs
As they gallop down to drink,
Shatter the golden roofs
Of the trees, for swift as the wind
They gallop down to the brink
Of the waters that echo their laughter,
Cavernous as rolling of boulders down hills;
Lolling, they lap at the gurgling waters.

. . . .

But nearer rises the sound,
Red, ragged as his comb,
Of a cock crowing;
A bird flies up to me at the window,
Leaping, like music, with regular rhythm,
Sinks down, then, to the city beneath.

3

Dressed, here, in bright colours,
The ants below are hurrying down the footways.
Under their various intolerable burdens
They stagger along.
Stop to converse, move, wave their antennæ.

. . . .

The fruit-seller is opening his stall,
Oranges are piled in minute pyramids,
While melons, green melons,
Swing from the roof in string cradles.
The butcher festoons his shop
With swags and gay wreaths of entrails;
Beautiful heads with horns,
Are nailed up, as on pagan altars
(Though their ears are fresh from the hearing

Of Orpheus playing his lute).
The Aguador arranges his glasses,
Out of which the sun will strike
His varying scales of crystal music
This afternoon, round the arena.
The Matador prepares for the fight,
Is, indeed, already in the tavern,
Where later and refreshed with blood,
He will celebrate his triumph
Among the poignant kindling
Of stringèd instruments.

. . . .

— But the child has run away crying;
I call — but no answer comes.

4

The chatter of the daylight grows
As I look upon the market-place,
Where there is a droning of bag-pipes,
And the hard, wooden music of the hills;
The housewife has left her cottage in the forest,
Driving here through the early tracks of the sun.
The beggars are already at their posts,
Their dry flesh peeps through their garments.
Their old ritual whining
Causes no show of pity.
Why should the hucksters, the busy people notice?
God himself has stood here, out at elbows,
Waiting patiently in the market-place,
While they chatter in gay booths.
But how I fear for them,
These who are not afraid!

I shout to them to make them understand.
They talk more, cease talking and look up,
They all look up, remain gaping.

. . . .

I went back into the water-cool room,
Put on my coloured coat, my buskin,
And mask of Harlequin.
They see me, this time.
"Come on, come on," they cry,
"You are just in time.
There is fun down here in the market-place.
Two men have been run over,
And there's to be a public execution.
The gallows are nearly up
— And after, in the evening,
We will go round the wineshops,
Strumming guitars,
While trills Dolores in her wide, red skirt.
Oh come on, come on!"
— But the paint from my mask runs down
And dyes my clothing.

5

It is not thus in the Northern cities,
Where the cold breathes close to the window-pane,
Where the brittle flowers of the frost
Crackle at the window's edge.
From my window in the Northern city
I can hear the rattle and roar of the town,
As the carts go lumbering over the bridges,
As the men in dark clothes hurry over the bridges.
They do not parade their hearts here,

They bury them at their lives' beginning.
They must hurry, or they will be late for their work;
Their work is their bread.
Without bread, how can they work?
They have no time for pleasure,
Nor is work any pleasure to them.
Their faces are masked with weariness,
Drab with their working.
(Only the tramp who moves among them
Unnoticed, despised,
Has eyes that have seen.)
They must work till the guns go again,
Giving them their only pretence to glory.
They have no time to fear,
No time to think of an end.
Foolishly I called to them on the bridges;
Only a few stopped, looked up
– But these were convulsed with fury.
Said one to another
"I have never seen a man
Behave like that before."
But most of them were mute;
They could not see.

. . . .

Through the murkiness of the Northern dawn,
The gas already flares out
In the glass palaces,
Where to-night, weary and dulled with smoke and with
drink,
They will seek, in a brief oblivion,
Laughter, and the mask of Ally Sloper.

. . . .

Thus it is in the Northern cities,
Where the cold lies close to the window-pane,
Where the grass grows its little blades of steel
And the wind is armed with seven whips.

6

Happy is Orpheus as he plays,
The dumb beasts listen quietly,
The music strokes their downy ears,
Melts the fierce fire within them.

Only with music can you tame the beasts,
Break them of their grizzly feasts;
Only with music can you open eyes to wonder.

. . . .

But if they will not hear?
The people have lost faith in music,
Few are there to call, and none to answer.

. . . .

When the Prince kissed the Sleeping Beauty,
He broke the wicked spell of cobwebs;
She answered, opened her eyes.

When Narcissus looked into the pool,
The cruel waters gave him their reply:
Even that was a better fate
Than to cry out in the lonely night
— And not to be answered.

7

From my high window in a Southern city,
One can see beyond the geometrical array

Of roofs, of Roman camps, now squares,
And intersecting streets,
Into far valleys;
Blue open flowers
Cupped between mountains.
The forests are so far away
They creep like humble green moss
Over mounds that are mountains.
But there, mid the deep penetrating glow
Of sunlight piercing through green leaves,
Sounds other music than the falling streams.

8

When Orpheus with his wind-swift fingers
Ripples the strings that gleam like rain,
The wheeling birds fly up and sing,
Hither, thither, echoing.
There is a crackling of dry twigs,
A sweeping of leaves along the ground.
Tawny faces and dumb eyes
Peer through unfluttering green screens
That mask ferocious teeth and claws,
Now tranquil.
As the music sighs upon the hills,
The young
Come skipping, ambling, rolling down,
Their soft ears flapping as they run,
Their fleecy coats catching in the thickets,
Till they lie, listening, round his feet.

. . . .

Unseen for centuries,
Fabulous creatures creep out of their caverns.

The Unicorn
Prances down from his bed of leaves,
His milk-white muzzle still stainèd green
With the munching, crunching of mountain herbs.
The Griffin usually so fierce,
Now tame and amiable again –
Has covered the bones in his secret cavern
With a rustling pall of dank, dead leaves,
While the Salamander – true lover of art –
Flickers, then creeps out of the flame;
Gently now, and away he goes,
Kindles his proud and blazing track
Across the forest,
Drawn to this melodious glade
Where, listening, he may cool his fever.

. . . .

When the housewife returns,
Carrying her basket,
She will not understand.
She misses nothing,
Has heard nothing in the woods.
She will only see
That the fire is dead,
The grate cold.

. . . .

But the child left in the empty house
Saw the Salamander leave the flame,
Heard a strange wind, like music, in the forest,
And has gone out to look for it,
Alone.

FOUR ITALIAN POEMS

Spring Morning

NOT so fine,
                But warm, oh warm
With an early smell of straw, of orris and of roses.

Listening clouds of sleep
Hang upon towers
As roses cling to walls,
Press the glistening flowers
Into the warm, damp earth again.

The little pigs squeal among the trodden straw,
The strawberries are sodden.
Under the eaves in the sweet, invisible rain
The birds chirp and gurgle in the gutters.

> "Is it fog that nuzzles my hand?"
> The old man mutters.
> "Damp and white is the fur of the old hunting dog,
> White and damp as fog,
> His coat smells of wet, but also of days that were good,
> When I was not stiff as wood in each bone
> And he slept less in the sun of an afternoon."

Summer

Sun dissolves to recreate.
Brick smoulders,
Plaster moulders
In the sun.
On the riven ground
The sweat of my labour falls all day like the rain.
Each night I die,
And in the morn am born again.
No time for my gun!
Yet I wipe my hair back from my forehead,
Look round me.
Not a bird in sight!
Flowers blow: mountains show:
Fruit and sky grow and glow.

What is the day's heat,
In the summer's husk?
Men calling in the fields,
Wheels creaking through the buzz and hum of summer.
But at night, in the heart of the heat,
The sounds are different,
Whether dry or glutinous;
The rhythmical, high shuffle of the cicada among the grasses,
The cool, cold-blooded cry of hunting owls
Who float and flap luminously in the darkness
And over all, that primal chant of earth,
The frogs, within their thick and mottled skins,
Croaking their common sense, croaking
In patches of warm wet darkness,

Lost in the universe;
Voices that only die when the chant of the priest begins,
After the day's first burst of tumbling, grumbling bells.

Autumn

The moth hums under the beams
In the darkened rooms,
Cool in their darkness, enclosed in autumn's glow
As the stone of the peach is bitter within the sweet flesh.

The moth hums and hovers under the rafters.
And below, men sing as they swing the oar of the wine-press,
Till the sharp juice spurts on the pavement and dyes it,
And the acrid scent sours the air,
Crisp and blue with the smoke of bonfires.

Now my dog whines to be out,
And we go with my gun,
Walking stiffly into the light of the evening, the light of the
        mountains,
Into the very eye of the sun,
    Until as I hide, to aim,
    The cypress and I grow one.

Winter

Rime lies crisp upon the ground,
But not in the great marshes.
There, the angry snout of the boar
Brushes aside the rushes.

In villages, tilted upon hills,
The swarthy, innocent-faced shepherds
Squeal on their wooden trumpets,
Squeak on their bagpipes,
Before the gold-haloed Virgin.

On the hills, under flat-topped pines,
The flames that were lit by the resting huntsmen,
Die like stars in a moment's sunshine
And leave a glistening ring upon the earth.

Part Three

POEMS OF THE WARS

TO CHARLOTTE CORDAY

OH, Huntsman, when will the hunting stop;
And the spring begin;
And the first star-eyed blossoms
Sprinkle earth's dull skin,
And Man's sorrow be again
Of divine ordination,
Not this evil, dull fruit
Of Man's negation?

In all lands under wide skies found
Men turn down the light and burrow
Like moles in the ground;
Only bully, bore and busybody
In beetle-armour clad
Scuttle round and hurry round
With hearts that are glad.

Has no man the courage to forbid it,
Now that the hounds are so near;
Has all the world no man to rid it
Of the hearts that have caused this fear,
Of the icy hearts and the bragging voices,
So that all the world rejoices
In a day when death was dear?

FOOL'S SONG

YESTERDAY is my To-morrow!
Private joy and private sorrow
Fade out of sight;
(Light, light, more light!)

The grin of the skull
Is now void and null,
Leaving no laughter
To float after.

(Echo cries " 'skull . . . dull, dull,'
Of fools is the world full,
Leaving hereafter
Matter for slaughter!")

Did you see — I saw — a tear
Falling, falling from King Lear,
No moisture giving,
Dry and perfect pearl of steel?

It fell, I tell you, to assuage
The nations that rage,
Mad as he, in wracking fear.
Do *you* think him mad, old Lear,

Because his eyes should thus sweat steel,
Icy, hard and without feel,
That, falling, whizzing, polished round
Can dig his own deep grave in ground?

. . . .

Hollow, my love, hollow your eye
And fie for your bony thigh, fie!
Let me count yours — I'm alive! —
Fingers, one, two, three, four, five!

Let me thank you, as I trace
All your elegance and grace,
Let me thank you for your smile
That will last so long a while.

BEFORE the last few individuals
Are staked upon the ant-heaps
For the dear little creatures to devour,
Let me recapitulate;

I hate high deeds
Mid high, aspiring words,
The bellow of old, blowsy buffaloes.
I love the beauty of the flowering meads
And sun-baked shepherds piping to their herds,
And waters lapping old walls, gold and rose.

I hate the clamorous voices of the crowd,
Its call for all to sacrifice for ever,
Abhor the dronings of its limpet leaders.
I love the quiet talk of those endowed
With reason — call it treason — ; the endeavour
To live and love. I hate the million readers

(I love their money, but shall see it never).
I love the panther on its stealthy paws
Leaping from past to future in streaked flash.
I love to prick the bubbles, and to sever
The laws that clutter up effect with cause,
To trip the clown and then to see him crash.

I love the peasant's earth-old cunning,
The look of all things bred from a long line,
And talk up in the air, upon the ladders.
I hate the boasting first, and then the running,

The blatant brag and then regretful whine,
The bloated money-bags that burst like bladders.

I hate war's busy beetles all arrayed
In dung-bright armour of old truth outworn.
I hate the clicking tongues within accustomed grooves,
I love speech to be bitter as a blade,
The unicorn with his rare ivory horn
And centaurs charging crowds with thundering hooves.

ENGLISH GOTHIC

Above the valley drifts a fleet
Of white, small clouds. Like castanets
The corn-crakes clack; down in the street
Old ladies air their canine pets.

The bells boom out with grumbling tone
To warn the people of the place
That soon they'll find upon His Throne
Their Maker, with a frowning face.

. . . . . .

The souls of bishops, shut in stone
By masons, rest in quietude:
As flies in amber, they atone
Each buzzing long-dead platitude.

For lichen plants its golden flush
Here, where the gaiter should have bent;
With glossy wings the black crows brush
Carved mitres, caw in merriment.

Wings blacker than a verger's hat
Beat on the air. These birds must learn
Their preaching note by pecking at
The lips of those who, treading fern,

Ascend the steps to Heaven's height.
— The willow herb, down by the wood,
Flares out to mark the phoenix-flight
Of God Apollo's car. Its hood

Singes the trees. The swans who float
— Wings whiter than the foam of sea —
Up the episcopal smooth moat,
Uncurl their necks to ring for tea.

. . . . . .

At this sign, in the plump green close
The Deans say grace. A hair pomade
Scents faded air. But still outside
Stone bishops scale a stone façade.

A thousand strong, church-bound, they look
Across shrill meadows — but to find
The cricket bat defeats the Book
— Matter triumphant over Mind!

Wellington said Waterloo
Was won upon the playing-fields;
Which thought might comfort clergy who
Applaud the virtues that rank yields.

But prelates of stone cannot relate
An Iron Duke's strong and silent words.
The knights in armour rest in state
Within, and grasp their marble swords.

Above, where flutter angel-wings
Caught in the organ's rolling loom,
Hang in the air, like jugglers' rings,
Dim quatrefoils of coloured gloom.

Tall arches rise to imitate
The jaws of Jonah's whale. Up flows

The chant. Thin spinsters sibilate
Beneath a full-blown Gothic rose.

Pillars surge upward, break in spray
Upon the high and fretted roof;
But children scream outside — betray
The urging of a cloven hoof.

. . . .

Tier above tier the Bishops stare
Away, away, . . . above the hills;
Their faded eyes repel the glare
Of dying sun, till sunset fills

Each pointed niche, in which they stand,
With glory of earth; humanity
Is spurned by one, with upturned hand,
Who warns them all is vanity.

The swan beneath the sunset arch
Expands his wings, as if to fly.
A thousand saints upon the march
Glow in the water — but to die.

A man upon the hill can hear
The organ. Echoes he has found
That, having lost religious fear,
Are pagan; till the rushing sound

Clearly denotes Apollo's car,
That roars past moat and bridge and tree,
The Young God sighs. . . . How far, how far,
Before the night shall set him free?

HOW SHALL WE RISE TO GREET THE DAWN?

How shall we rise to greet the dawn,
Not timidly,
With a hand before our eyes?

. . . .

We will welcome the strong light
Joyfully:
Nor will we mistake the dawn
For the mid-day.

We must create and fashion a new God —
A God of power, of beauty, and of strength —
Created painfully, cruelly,
Labouring from the revulsion of men's minds.

It is not only that the money-changers
Ply their trade
Within the sacred places;
But that the old God
Has made the Stock Exchange his Temple.
We must drive him from it.
Why should we tinker with clay feet?
We will fashion
A perfect unity
Of precious metals.

Let us tear the paper moon
From its empty dome.
Let us see the world with young eyes.
Let us harness the waves to make power,
And in so doing,

Seek not to spoil their rolling freedom,
But to endow
The soiled and straining cities
With the same splendour of strength.

We will not be afraid,
Though the golden geese cackle in the Capitol,
In fear
Lest their eggs may be placed
In an incubator.

. . . .

Continually they cackle thus,
These venerable birds,
Crying, "Those whom the Gods love
Die young"
Or something of that sort.
But we will see that they live
And prosper.

Let us prune the tree of language
Of its dead fruit.
Let us melt up the clichés
Into molten metal,
Fashion weapons that will scald and flay;
Let us curb this eternal humour
And become witty.
Let us dig up the dragon's teeth
From this fertile soil
Swiftly,
Before they fructify;
Let us give them as medicine
To the writhing monster itself.

. . . .

We must create and fashion a new God—
A God of power, of beauty, and of strength;
Created painfully, cruelly,
Labouring from the revulsion of men's minds.
Cast down the idols of a thousand years,
Crush them to dust
Beneath the dancing rhythm of our feet.
Oh! let us dance upon the weak and cruel:
We must create and fashion a new God.

"THEREFORE IS THE NAME OF IT CALLED BABEL"

AND still we stood and stared far down
Into that ember-glowing town,
Which every shaft and shock of fate
Had shorn unto its base. Too late
  Came carelessly Serenity.

Now torn and broken houses gaze
On to the rat-infested maze
That once sent up rose-silver haze
  To mingle through eternity.

The outlines once so strongly wrought,
Of city walls, are now a thought
Or jest unto the dead who fought . . .
  Foundation for futurity.

The shimmering sands where once there played
Children with painted pail and spade,
Are drearly desolate — afraid
  To meet night's dark humanity,

Whose silver cool remakes the dead,
And lays no blame on any head
For all the havoc, fire, and lead,
  That fell upon us suddenly,

When all we came to know as good
Gave way to Evil's fiery flood,

And monstrous myths of iron and blood
  Seem to obscure God's clarity.

Deep sunk in sin, this tragic star
Sinks deeper still, and wages war
Against itself; strewn all the seas
With victims of a world disease
– And we are left to drink the lees
Of Babel's direful prophecy.

THE ETERNAL CLUB

WARMING their withered hands, the dotards say:
"In our youth men were happy till they died.
What is it ails the young men of to-day —
To make them bitter and dissatisfied?"
Two thousand years ago it was the same:
"Poor Joseph! How he'll feel about his son!
I knew him as a child — his head aflame
With gold, he seemed so full of life and fun.
And even as a young man he was fine,
Converting tasteless water into wine. . . .
Then something altered him. He tried to chase
The money-changers from the Temple door.
White ringlets swung and tears shone in their poor
Aged eyes. He grew so bitter and found men
For friends as discontented — lost all count
Of caste — denied his father, faith, and then
He preached that *dreadful* Sermon on the Mount!
Nor even after, would he let things be;
For when they nailed him high up on the tree,
And gave him vinegar, and pierced his side,
He asked God to forgive them — still dissatisfied!"

ARM-CHAIR

If I were now of handsome middle-age,
I should not govern yet, but still should hope
To help the prosecution of this war.
I'd talk and eat (though not eat wheaten bread),
I'd send my sons, if old enough, to France,
Or help to do my share in other ways.

All through the long spring evenings, when the sun
Pursued its primrose path toward the hills,
If fine, I'd plant potatoes on the lawn;
If wet, write anxious letters to the Press.
I'd give up wine and spirits, and with pride
Refuse to eat meat more than once a day,
And seek to rob the workers of their beer.
The only way to win a hard-fought war
Is to annoy the people in small ways,
Bully or patronize them, as you will!
I'd teach poor mothers, who have seven sons
— All fighting men of clean and sober life —
How to look after babies and to cook;
Teach them to save their money and invest;
Not to bring children up in luxury
— But do without a nursemaid in the house!

If I were old or only seventy,
Then should I be a great man in his prime.
I should rule army corps; at my command
Men would rise up, salute me, and attack
— And die. Or I might also govern men
By making speeches with my toothless jaws,
Constant in chatter, until men should say,
"One grand old man is still worth half his pay!"

That day, I'd send my grandsons out to France
– And wish I'd got ten other ones to send
(One cannot sacrifice too much, I'd say).
Then would I make a noble, toothless speech,
And all the list'ning Parliament would cheer.
"We cannot and we will not end this war
Till all the younger men with martial mien
Have enter'd capitals; never make peace
Till they are cripples, on one leg, or dead!"

Then would the Bishops go nigh mad with joy,
Cantuar, Ebor, and the other ones,
Be overwhelmed with pious ecstasy
In thanking Him we'd got a Christian,
An Englishman, still worth his salt, to talk.
In every pulpit would they preach and prance;
And our great Church would work, as heretofore,
To bring this poor old nation to its knees.
Then we'd forbid all liberty, and make
Free speech a relic of our impious past;
And when this war is finished, when the world
Is torn and bleeding, cut and bruised to death,
Then I'd pronounce my peace terms – to the poor!

. . . .

But as it is, I am not ninety yet,
And so must pay my reverence to these men –
These grand old men, who still can see and talk,
Who sacrifice each other's sons each day.
O Lord! let me be ninety yet, I pray.
Methuselah was quite a youngster when
He died. Now, vainly weeping, we should say:
"Another great man perished in his prime!"
O let me govern, Lord, at ninety-nine!

THE TRAP

THE world is young and green.
Its woods are golden beneath the May-time sun;
But within its trap of steel the rabbit plunges
Madly to and fro.
It will bleed to death
Slowly,
        Slowly,
Unless there is some escape.
Why will not someone release it?

And presently a kindly passer-by
Stoops down.
The rabbit's eye glints at him —
Gleaming from the impenetrable obscurity of its prison.
He stoops and lifts the catch
(He cannot hold it long, for the spring is heavy).
The rabbit could now be free,
But does not move;
For from the darkness of its death-hutch
The world looks like another brightly baited trap.
So, remaining within its steel prison,
It argues thus:
    "Perhaps I may bleed to death,
    But it will probably take a long time,
    And, at any rate,
    I am secure
    From the clever people outside.
    Besides, if I did come out now
    All the people who thought I was a lion
    Would see, by the trap-mark on my leg,

That I am only an unfortunate rabbit,
And this might promote disloyalty among the children.

. . . .

When the clamp closed on my leg
It was a ruse
To kill me,
So probably the lifting of it betrays the same purpose!
If I come out now
They will think they can trap rabbits
Whenever they like.
How do I know they will not snare me
Again next year?
Besides, it looks to me from here . . ."

But the catch drops down,
For the stranger is weary.
From within the hutch
A thin stream of blood
Trickles on to the grass
Outside,
And leaves a brown stain on its brightness.
But the dying rabbit is happy,
Saying:
"I knew it was only a trap!"

HYMN TO MOLOCH

HOLY Moloch, blessèd lord,
Hatred to our souls impart!
Put the heathen to the sword,
Wound and pierce each contrite heart.
Never more shall darkness fall
But it seem a funeral pall;
Never shall the red sun rise
But to red and swollen eyes.
In the centuries that roll,
Slowly grinding out our tears,
Often Thou hast taken toll;
Never till these latter years
Have *all* nations lost the fray;
Lead not Thou our feet astray.

Never till the present time
Have we offered all we hold,
With one gesture, mad, sublime,
Sons and lovers, lands and gold.
Must we, then, still pray to Thee,
Moloch, for a victory?

Eternal Moloch, strong to slay,
Do not seek to heal or save.
Lord, it is the better way
Swift to send them to the grave.
Those of us too old to go
Send our sons to face the foe,
But, O lord! *we* must remain
Here, to pray and sort the slain.

In every land the widows weep,
In every land the children cry.
Other gods are lulled to sleep,
All the starving peoples die.
What is left to offer Thee?
Thou, O Sacred King of Death!
God of Blood and Lord of Guile,
Do not let us waste our breath,
Cast on us Thy crimson smile,
Moloch, lord, we pray to Thee,
Send at least *one* victory.

All the men in every land
Pray to Thee through battle's din,
Swiftly now to show thy hand,
Pray that soon one side may win.
Under sea and in the sky,
Everywhere our children die;
Laughter, happiness and light
Perished in a single night.

In every land the heaving tides
Wash the sands a dreadful red,
In every land the tired sun hides
Under heaps and hills of dead,
In spite of all we've offered up
Must we drink and drain the cup?
Everywhere the dark floods rise,
Everywhere our hearts are torn.
Every day a new Christ dies,
Every day a devil's born.
Moloch, lord, we pray to Thee,
Send at least *one* victory.

OLD–FASHIONED SPORTSMEN

WE thank thee,
O Lord,
That the War is over.
We can now
Turn our attention
Again
To money-making.
Railway-Shares must go up;
Wages must come down;
Smoke shall come out
Of the chimneys of the North,
And we will manufacture battle-ships.
    We thank thee, O Lord,
    But we must refuse
    To consider
    Music, Painting, or Poetry.

Our sons and brothers
Went forth to fight,
To kill certain things,
Cubism, Futurism and Vers-libre.
    "All this Poetry-and-Rubbish,"
    We said,
    "Will not stand the test of war."
We will not read a book
– Unless it is a best seller.
There has been enough art
In the past,
Life is concerned
With killing and maiming.

If they cannot kill men,
Why can't they kill animals?
There is still
Big Game in Africa
— Or there might be trouble
Among the natives.
    We thank thee, O Lord,
    But we will not read poetry.

But as the Pharisees
Approached the tomb
They saw the boulder
Rolled back,
And that the tomb was empty.
— They said:
    "It's very disconcerting.
    I am not at all
    Narrow-minded.
    I know a tune
    When I hear one,
    And I know
    What I like —
    I did not so much mind
    That He blasphemed,
    Saying that He was the Son-of-God,
    But He was never, well,
    What I call
    A Sportsman;
    For forty days
    He went out into the desert
    — And never shot anything:
    And when we hoped He would drown,
    He walked on the waters."

CORPSE–DAY

(*July 19th, 1919* *)

Dusk floated up from the earth beneath,
Held in the arms of the evening wind
— The evening wind that softly creeps
Along the jasper terraces,
To bear with it
The old, sad scent
Of midsummer, of trees and flowers
Whose bell-shaped blossoms, shaken, torn
By the rough fingers of the day,
Ring out their frail and honeyed notes.

. . . .

Up from the earth there rose
Sounds of great triumph and rejoicing.

. . . .

Our Lord Jesus, the Son of Man,
Smiled
And leant over the ramparts of Heaven.
Beneath Him
Through the welling clouds of darkness
He could see
The swarming of mighty crowds.

It was in the Christian Continent,
Especially,
That the people chanted
Hymns and pæans of joy.
But it seemed to Our Lord
That through the noisy cries of triumph

* The official celebration of Peace.

He could still detect
A bitter sobbing
— The continuous weeping of widows and children
Which had haunted Him for so long,
Though He saw only
The bonfires,
The arches of triumph,
The processions,
And the fireworks
That soared up
Through the darkening sky,
To fall in showers of flame
Upon the citadel of Heaven.
As a rocket burst,
There fell from it,
Screaming in horror,
Hundreds of men
Twisted into the likeness of animals
— Writhing men
Without feet,
Without legs,
Without arms,
Without faces. . . .

The earth-cities still rejoiced.
Old, fat men leant out to cheer
From bone-built palaces.
Gold flowed like blood
Through the streets;
Crowds became drunk
On liquor distilled from corpses.
And peering down

The Son of Man looked into the world;
He saw
That within the churches and the temples
His image had been set up;
But, from time to time,
Through twenty centuries,
The priests had touched up the countenance
So as to make war more easy
Or intimidate the people —
Until now the face
Had become the face of Moloch!
The people did not notice
The change
. . . But Jesus wept!

THE NEXT WAR

THE long war had ended.
Its miseries had grown faded.
Deaf men became difficult to talk to,
Heroes became bores.

Those alchemists
Who had converted blood into gold
Had grown elderly.
But they held a meeting,
Saying,
"We think perhaps we ought
To put up tombs
Or erect altars
To those brave lads
Who were so willingly burnt,
Or blinded,
Or maimed,
Who lost all likeness to a living thing,
Or were blown to bleeding patches of flesh
For our sakes.
It would look well.
Or we might even educate the children."
But the richest of these wizards
Coughed gently,
And he said:

> "I have always been to the front
> — In private enterprise —
> I yield in public spirit
> To no man.
> I think yours is a very good idea

— A capital idea —
And not too costly. . . .
But it seems to me
That the cause for which we fought
Is again endangered.
What more fitting memorial for the fallen
Than that their children
Should fall for the same cause?"

Rushing eagerly into the street,
The kindly old gentleman cried
To the young:
"Will you sacrifice
Through your lethargy
What your fathers died to gain?
The world *must* be made safe for the young!"

. . . .

And the children
Went. . . .

November 1918

ASPIRING APE

I love in man the ape, and not the angel,
The transience that clothes abiding bones!
Kin to the sun and earth, to green things growing,
He's not content — oh torment of time flowing! —
With dusty chanting before timeless thrones.

To man, the ape has given love and courage,
Dexterity and patience, wit and fire,
A nameless aching of the heart with wonder,
That humble, idiot longing to aspire
Which blossoms in the arts' vast world of thunder.

Where did the angel lurk in Helen of Troy!
(The monkey's skull was structure for her beauty.)
What does the angel bring for our fulfilling,
Except a sense of righteousness in killing,
And brag of abnegation and of duty?

To man, the monkey brings an animal warmth,
The lovely gift of life not everlasting,
And talk and laughter and the seeing eyes;
So let no man this ancestor despise,
Who brings the arts, the customs and the trades,
And when he kills, talks never of crusades!

A ROSE IN THE MOUTH

In his *Journals* for 1896, André Gide mentions that Francis Jammes gave him his own walking-stick; on which were carved, lengthwise, various verses. Among them were the lines: "*Un écureuil avait une rose à la bouche, Un âne le traita de fou.*"

"WHY do you climb the trees with a rose in your mouth,
When you might be down here with me, eating the grass;
How can you dream of the scented, the lily-long lazy south,
When you might be collecting and numbering nuts in the
  north
For a winter that has no end?" asked the ass.

Said the squirrel, "My nuts are the stars:
Towards them I climb. You are clamped to the earth.
In a moment I'll pelt you with planets, with Mars
And with Venus, till even you see
Why *I* wear a rose in my mouth!

Only a symbol, the rose in my mouth,"
Mocked the squirrel.
"My heart *is* a rose. I've a rose in my blood as well,
And the top of my tree, my ivory tower, discloses
The whole of the world as valleys and mountains of roses."

"No! The world is a map made solely for ant and for ass,
For I roll, and thus from the feel of my fur, I can tell,"
Brayed the donkey, "We offer no flowers, only grass,
With blood, sweat and tears; then a shroud,
And the cheers of the crowd."

"My heart *is* a rose," repeated the leaping squirrel,
"I've a rose in my blood as well!"
But the rose in his mouth was the blood
As he fell.